Original title:
Primrose Promises

Copyright © 2025 Creative Arts Management OÜ
All rights reserved.

Author: Samuel Kensington
ISBN HARDBACK: 978-1-80566-765-0
ISBN PAPERBACK: 978-1-80566-835-0

Canvas of Awakened Souls

In a world where daisies conspire,
To paint the skies a shade of dire,
A jolly bee buzzes with glee,
Wearing glasses, as cool as can be.

Silly squirrels play hopscotch with sprigs,
While rabbits in hats dance jigs,
They sing of the day and the night,
In the garden where laughter is bright.

Sunrays on a Petal's Dream

A sunflower's hat is quite absurd,
It sways and spins, oh how it stirred!
Ladybugs hold a fashion show,
With polka dots, they steal the show.

The wind whispers secrets so slight,
As petals pirouette with delight,
A froggy chorus croaks out a tune,
Underneath the chuckling moon.

The Promise of Tomorrow's Bloom

Seeds giggle as they dream of the light,
Hoping to sprout in the warm sunlight,
A dandelion gives a cheery cheer,
As pollen floats, spreading some cheer.

Ants march in lines, all in a hurry,
They trip on a stick and start to flurry,
Reminding us all, take life slow,
Even the busy need a show.

Harmony Beneath the Boughs

Under the trees where shadows play,
Laughter lingers through the day,
A wise old owl with a wry little grin,
Talks nonsense, but sparks a spin.

Chipmunks chatter, plotting a game,
To win the award for the quirkiest name,
As branches sway with a gentle laugh,
They all come together for a silly photograph.

The Soft Glow of New Beginnings

In gardens where laughter spills,
Tiny blooms play hide and seek.
With every petal, a ticklish thrill,
They giggle beneath the sun's warm cheek.

When buds burst open, oh what a sight,
They dance with bees in their giddy spree.
Colorful hats in morning light,
Wiggling roots as carefree as can be.

The Music of Late Blossoms

Tiny trumpets in the breeze,
Swaying gently, they sing a tune.
With bumbles and giggles, they aim to please,
Making laughter bloom under the moon.

Each blossom wears a silly grin,
They can't help but chuckle together.
As petals twirl and spin, spin, spin,
They spread joy like fluffy feather.

A Realm of Colorful Whispers

In a kingdom where daisies sway,
Secrets flutter on butterfly wings.
They whisper tales of a sunny day,
While ants trot along with tiny blings.

A riot of colors, all dressed up,
They joke about the bees' silly flight.
With every breeze, they lift their cup,
Toasting to each smile, pure delight.

Enchantment in Every Leaf

Leaves giggle softly, tell their tales,
Of rainy days and sunny cheer.
They tickle toes and flutter sails,
As the squirrel nods with a wink and a leer.

In the shade, where shadows play,
Tree branches dance with a jolly twist.
Each rustling sound seems to say,
Join the fun, you can't resist!

Secrets Beneath the Blossoms

In the garden, whispers grow,
Mice are planning quite a show.
With acorn hats and twiggy gear,
They dance and giggle, glad we're near.

Flowers nod and share a joke,
Sunlight beams, and shadows poke.
Worms exchange the juiciest tales,
While buzzing bees wear tiny veils.

Echoes of Spring's Awakening

The frogs croak symphonies loud and proud,
While butterflies twirl, a colorful crowd.
The bunnies race with carrots to claim,
As ladybugs cheer and chant their name.

Tulips sway in breezy delight,
While ants march various ways, such a sight!
They argue over crumbs and crumbs of bread,
"Mine is better!"—hops the one with dread.

Petals Unfurled at Dusk

As night creeps in with starlit grace,
Crickets chirp, creating a bass.
Blooming flowers hold a feast,
Laughter echoes, not a moment ceased.

Owl hoots a riddle, clever and sly,
Chasing moths, who ballet and fly.
"Guess who's here?"—snores the big fat toad,
"Wake me when the moonlight's glowed!"

A Promise in Each Blossom

Beneath each bud, a secret beam,
Dancing fairies, or so it seems.
With tiny shoes and laughter bright,
They twirl together in the moonlight.

Daisies giggle and tell of dreams,
While tulips wear their fancy seams.
"Will it rain?" asks the shy little sprout,
Only to hear, "Yes, that's what it's about!"

Echoes of Nature's Tender Pledge

In a garden where giggles grow,
Bumblebees dance in a quirky show.
Worms wear hats and sing a tune,
Mice hold meetings beneath the moon.

Flowers gossip, petals sway,
Dandelions wish the clouds would play.
Grass tickles toes that wander near,
Laughter floats in the golden sphere.

Butterflies wiggle, trying to chat,
While frogs in chorus croak and spat.
Sunshine spills, like spilled hot tea,
Oh, nature's antics, wild and free!

With every bloom, a jest unfolds,
As whispers of joy our heart beholds.
In this patch, where whimsy thrives,
Nature chuckles while it jives.

The Language of Fresh Beginnings

Morning splashes colors bright,
Dewdrops dance in pure delight.
Squirrels chatter with a wink,
As sunbeams poke, "Time to blink!"

Rabbits bounce with silly flair,
Clouds float by without a care.
Trees giggle in the gentle breeze,
"Come join our playful, leafy tease!"

Seeds exchange their best-kept plans,
"Let's sprout joy!" say tiny fans.
In every corner, life's a jest,
Where nature's laughter knows no rest.

With each dawn, a prank's reborn,
In this world, we laugh 'til worn.
For every bud that dares to peek,
Nature winks, "We're all unique!"

Dreams Wrapped in Dewdrops

Under skies of cotton fluff,
Bees play tag; they can't get enough.
Raindrops giggle on petals fine,
Nature's dreams weave, oh-so-divine.

Caterpillars in top hats prance,
Throw a party, give chance a glance.
Bubbles burst with a pop and cheer,
Join the fun, it's time, my dear!

Ladybugs train in marching lines,
While ants debate on silly signs.
Every dewdrop holds a tale,
As whispers glide on the breeze's sail.

Each dawn unfolds a brand new jest,
Wrapped in laughs, life feels its best.
In every leaf, a chuckle's stored,
Nature's secrets never bored.

Beneath the Surface of Hope

In the pond where frogs debate,
They croak out jokes about a plate.
Goldfish giggle, swim so fast,
Fleeting jokes are flung and cast.

Snails race with shells that gleam,
Chasing dreams on a shiny beam.
Underneath the lily's guise,
Laughter bubbles, surprise, surprise!

Marshmallows float in a sugar spree,
While turtles ponder, "What's the key?"
Colors dance beneath moon's glow,
In this watery world, playfulness flows.

Each ripple holds a tease from fate,
Beneath the surface, joy awaits.
For every splash and every note,
Nature's humor weaves and floats.

Nature's Silent Surrender

In the garden, a squirrel prances,
Chasing shadows, he takes chances.
Whispers giggle in breezy trees,
Nature laughs, her heart at ease.

The flowers blush, the bees are buzzing,
In their dance, the earth is fussing.
Earthworms wiggle, doing a jig,
While the frogs croak, flamingo-rig.

Sunset drapes in pastel dresses,
While rabbits hop in fancy guests.
Every creature seems to jest,
Nature's comedy, we find the best.

Morning dew, like diamonds bright,
Paves the path for playful flight.
With every bloom, humor's alive,
The world laughs, and we all thrive.

Petal-Kissed Reveries

A buttercup wears a golden crown,
While daisies spin in a floral gown.
The wind tells tales of silly clowns,
As butter on toast in a picnic frown.

Ants march on in military style,
With crumbs that make us all smile.
Ladybugs dance on a leaf parade,
While spiders craft a wobbly trade.

Moonbeams giggle, casting light,
As fireflies blink to the starry night.
Nature's glimmer is pure delight,
In every petal, a comic sight.

The daisies wink with each passing breeze,
As bumblebees sing their buzzing tease.
Silly as socks without a pair,
Nature's poems float in the air.

Beneath the Skies of New Beginnings

The dawn breaks with a sip of tea,
Where hummingbirds hover with glee.
Sunshine stretches, yawns in delight,
Morning's circus is quite the sight.

Clouds wear hats, fluffy and bright,
As bunnies bounce in frolicsome flight.
Each drop of dew is a giggling cheer,
While the meadows whisper, 'Spring is here!'

Grass tickles toes in playful tease,
With daisies prancing in the breeze.
Nature chuckles with gentle grace,
Each moment's laugh is a warm embrace.

Tadpoles splish in a watery game,
As butterflies dodge and tease their name.
In this world of whimsy, let's play along,
For every heartbeat sings a silly song.

Lullabies to the Awakening Earth

Crickets croon to the moonlit skies,
While sleepy flowers close their eyes.
A snail slides by on a glimmering trail,
Wearing a shell like a ship's detailed sail.

The nightingale sings a tune so sweet,
While hedgehogs shuffle their wobbly feet.
Stars twinkle, laughing at the show,
As shadows prance, putting on a glow.

Pollen drifts in a gentle breeze,
Sprinkling dreams beneath the trees.
The earth giggles, a lullaby soft,
As sleepy heads begin to loft.

Morning will come with a wink and a grin,
Awakening secrets held deep within.
Nature hums as the day starts anew,
In harmony, expect a chuckle or two.

Remnants of Color in Evening Light

In the dusk, colors play,
Flowers giggle, come what may.
Bees wear tiny party hats,
While laughing at the snoozing cats.

Petals whisper, what a sight,
Stars start winking, oh so bright.
A daisy dares to twirl around,
Where sun and silly shadows abound.

Grass tries tickling sleepy toes,
A dance party in a garden grows.
Mice in bow ties stomp the ground,
In this twilight ball, joy is found.

The Promise of Tomorrow's Bloom

Seeds hold secrets, burrowed tight,
They dream of colors, quite a sight.
Tomorrow's blooms will surely tease,
As they flutter in the breeze.

In the soil, a loud giggle,
Tiny sprouts begin to wiggle.
They promise love will soon increase,
In petals soft, they find their peace.

With sunlit dresses made of cheer,
Bees and bugs will soon reappear.
A chorus sings, they cannot wait,
For blooms to join this funny fate.

Melodies of a Garden in Love

Crickets strum their nightly tunes,
As flowers dance beneath the moons.
Love blooms silly in the air,
Petals twirl without a care.

Oh, bees hum sweet serenades,
While daisies plot their grand charades.
The sun flirts with a passing cloud,
In the garden, laughter's loud.

Butterflies play hide and seek,
They gossip softly, oh so chic.
Nature's band starts to provide,
Joyful tunes where fun won't hide.

Pages from the Botanical Diary

Once upon a leafy page,
Where flowers dream of center stage.
Petunia writes with ink so bright,
Of butterflies that danced in flight.

The sun held hands with silly rain,
Creating puddles in the lane.
A snapdragon tells a jest,
Blooming daily is its quest.

The daisies wish to pen their tales,
About the wind and happy gales.
In this diary, laughter rings,
In gardens filled with wildest things.

Tender Threads of Life

In gardens where the giggles sprout,
The threads of life twist about.
A worm in dance, a bee with flair,
Who knew bugs could have such hair?

The daisies laugh, they sway and beam,
While petals curl like ice cream dreams.
With muddy paws and joyful yells,
The garden's chaos, all is well.

Tiny fairies lose their hats,
Chasing butterflies and chubby cats.
Each bloom a joke, a playful tease,
In nature's jest, we find our ease.

So let the laughter fill the air,
With every color, every dare.
For in this patch of sun and cheer,
Life's funny threads draw us near.

Bright Eyes in a Floral Sea

In fields of colors, bright and bold,
With eyes that sparkle, tales unfold.
A bunny plays peek-a-boo with me,
In this floral ocean, wild and free.

The sunflowers wave like giant friends,
While ladybugs spin and make amends.
A dandelion giggles in the breeze,
As fluffy clouds float with such ease.

Here's a bee stuck in a rose,
Not sure if it's work or a pose.
And butterflies wear sparkly gowns,
While grasshoppers dance, flipping upside down.

In this garden, the laughter flows,
With every bloom, the joy just grows.
Together we twirl, spin round and round,
In this floral sea where fun is found.

Nourishing the Seeds of Hope

Dirt cakes and watermelons, oh my!
Planting dreams beneath the sky.
A silly squirrel stole my cap,
Leaving me with a muddy map.

A sprout peeks out with a curious grin,
It tickles my nose with a gentle spin.
With every seed sown, a giggle grows,
In the dirt of dreams where laughter flows.

Rainbows dance with raindrops bright,
As worms dress up for a fancy night.
Each blade of grass, a story to tell,
In nature's nursery, all is swell.

So plant your hopes and watch them sprout,
In gardens of laughter, without a doubt.
For every flower that brightly glows,
Is a bouquet of joy that truly overflows.

Whispers in the Meadow

In whispers soft, the daisies chat,
About the moon, the sun, and that silly cat.
Grass blades tickle puppy noses,
As giggling children share their roses.

The butterflies hold secret meets,
Exchanging gossip on fluffy seats.
While ants parade with a tiny drum,
Creating melodies, here they come!

Oh, listen close to the flower tunes,
As the breeze hums low under the moons.
A clownish gopher juggles peas,
In a meadow where joy is a breeze.

So dance along with the wildflowers,
And let laughter bloom in joyful hours.
In this meadow, let spirits soar,
For each whisper binds us evermore.

Effervescence After the Rain

Puddles laugh with muddy glee,
A splashing dance from you to me.
Rubber ducks parade around,
While raindrops play a silly sound.

Umbrellas spin like wedding cakes,
As umbrellas flip and laughter wakes.
We jump in streams with silly flair,
Who knew the clouds could pull a scare?

Giggles rise like bubbles in tea,
Dancing droplets, carefree spree.
With every stomp, the joy we find,
A puddle kingdom, rain's rewind.

So here we splash, no need for sighs,
Embracing joy 'neath gloomy skies.
In our wet world, we become bold,
A rainy tale that never gets old.

A Dance Among the Foliage

Leaves are twirling in delight,
Swinging high beneath the light.
A squirrel joins with acorn hat,
While birds giggle, 'What's up with that?'

Trees are swaying, roots like feet,
Nature's groove is quite the treat.
Frogs wear tuxedos, making a scene,
While dandelions spin, looking keen.

In the grass, a waltz takes flight,
Beetles jive, oh what a sight!
Mice do the cha-cha, all aglow,
As flowers dance in a lively show.

Wind plays tunes on nature's strings,
A happy chorus that laughter brings.
Join the fun 'neath the leafy throne,
For it's not just plants that dance alone.

The Tapestry of Innocence

Stitches of giggles, threads of cheer,
A quilt of joy, so pure and dear.
Blankets woven with childhood dreams,
Whimsical patterns, nothing as it seems.

Buttons smile like old pals do,
While yarn snakes wrap, jovial too.
Knitting tales of silly woes,
At every loop, a laughter grows.

In this cozy world, we play pretend,
Where make-believe has no end.
A teddy bear sips tea so fine,
As we twirl tales on a sunny line.

Crayons drawing, colors collide,
In a riot of hues, we take a ride.
Each stitch tugs at a mile-wide grin,
For childhood's laughter starts within.

Promises Woven in Green

In the meadow, sprouts of mirth,
Silly secrets hide beneath earth.
Worms wear glasses, wise and spry,
As daisies wink and sway nearby.

The breeze tickles the blades of grass,
As butterflies dance, chubby and crass.
Their flights are bumbles, oh what a sight,
In a swirl of colors, pure delight!

Fairies giggle from the daffodils,
While laughter bubbles up from the hills.
Each flower whispers a funny riddle,
As critters gather 'round for a twiddle.

Nature's symphony, playful and grand,
With each giggle, the world expands.
In this garden where whimsy resides,
The playful heart forever abides.

The Heartbeat of the Earth

Beneath the ground, the worms all dance,
With each small wiggle, they take a chance.
The roots are gossiping, oh what a sight,
Silly stories from morning till night.

The daisies giggle, the tulips tease,
While grumpy old thorns stab at the breeze.
A uproar of laughter spills through the leaves,
As petals trade secrets, like whispers of thieves.

The sun casts shadows, the clouds play too,
Making faces that change with each hue.
Nature's a comedian, what a great show,
Each plant a performer, stealing the glow.

So dance little daisies, shake off your fears,
Let laughter ring out, come join in the cheers!
For in this green theater, under the sky,
The heartbeat of earth is a comedic sigh.

Journeys in a Flower's Dream

In a flower's dream, the bees wear hats,
While butterflies gossip with chubby chitchats.
One flower declared, 'I'm planning a trip!'
With petals all packed, it started to slip.

The ladybugs chuckled, 'Let's follow the breeze,
Adventure awaits in the tall oak trees.'
With a flutter and flap, they set off to roam,
A caravan of colors, they felt quite at home.

But the journey was tricky, a slippery route,
With puddles of dew that made petals shoot!
They slipped and they slid, their laughter rang clear,
A flower's great dream filled with giggles and cheer.

With each little tumble, they laughed all the more,
For every mishap opened a door.
In the heart of the garden, they found their way,
In a journey of joy that would brighten the day.

Between the Stems of Hope

Between the stems where the critters convene,
The grasshoppers dance in a jovial scene.
While ladybugs boast of their 'spotty' success,
And beetles just grin in shiny finesse.

A weary old sunflower signs with a frown,
Complaining of flowers that never sit down.
'Back in my day, we just blinked in the sun,'
So loud blooms ignore him, and frolic for fun.

The clovers are plotting a mischievous game,
Where flowers get tangled and yell out each name.
A playful retreat hides under the leaves,
While blooms trade their stories and giggle in eves.

So join in their laughter, don't miss out the cheer,
For between the stems of hope, joy draws near.
In the garden of giants, there's nothing to rue,
Just a festival of fun beneath skies so blue.

Stories Written by Nature's Hand

In the garden, tales unfold,
Where flowers gossip, bright and bold.
The daisies whisper, secrets shared,
While the tulips laugh, none are scared.

Bees buzz tales of sweet delight,
While butterflies take their flight.
A squirrel pranks a sleeping cat,
Nature writes stories, how about that?

The sunbeams dance on leafy pages,
Painting scenes from ancient ages.
With every bloom, there's joy bestowed,
As nature winks down the little road.

So let us listen, heed the call,
In blooms and whispers, there's fun for all.
Nature's stories, wild and true,
Always bring laughter, just for you.

In the Embrace of Blossoms

Amidst the petals, giggles grow,
When pollen dances, watch it flow.
Butterflies tease, oh what a sight,
In the embrace of color and light.

Daffodils chuckle, swaying with ease,
While bumblebees hum along with breeze.
The blossoms wear their bright summer hats,
And play peek-a-boo with the fluffy cats.

Tulips tiptoe, so bold and bright,
As the sun dips low, kissing goodnight.
Fragrance floats like a merry tune,
Making everyone sway like a cartoon.

Here joy blooms with each little cheer,
Nature's laughter is more than clear.
In this garden, nonsense reigns supreme,
A whimsical, flowery daydream.

Visions of Tomorrow

With every seed that takes its flight,
Dreams of tomorrow dance in the light.
Laughter sprouts where daisies lean,
In the garden of hope, bright and green.

The grass tickles with every breeze,
While ladybugs play hide and tease.
Snails take their time, making a plan,
"Step by step, we are nature's fans!"

Buds unfurl, revealing delight,
As worms compose their nightly flight.
In this realm of bliss and charm,
The world spins fast, but we stay warm.

So let us gather, laugh, and grow,
In the visions that nature will show.
Tomorrow is bright, with mischief afoot,
Under the sky, where laughter is put.

A Melody of Blossoms

In gardens where giggles bloom and sway,
Nature's orchestra plays every day.
The lilies tap dance, heels click and clack,
While echoes of joy bounce back and track.

Sunflowers reach for the high notes,
As bumblebees hum in cute little boats.
Roses croon sweetly, teasing the breeze,
They'll sing you a song, if you bring some cheese!

Winds play the flute, rustling leaves,
Creating a symphony that never deceives.
In this melody, let your heart sing,
Join in the fun that the blossoms bring.

From morning till dusk, let laughter flow,
In harmony where the wildflowers grow.
Nature's concert, a whimsical flight,
With blossoms composing delight day and night.

Soft Satin Blooms

In gardens where the colors mix,
A flower dons its silken tricks.
It sways and giggles, oh so spry,
Its petal dance can make you cry.

With little bees that buzz around,
They whisper secrets, quite profound.
"Is that a flower?" one bee grins,
"Or just a snack?" the laughter spins.

A soft gust blows, the blooms all sway,
As if to join the grand ballet.
With every twist and teasing tease,
They spark the joy of springtime breeze.

So if you see them, take a look,
These little jesters, nature's book.
They'll share their laughs and bloom-like cheer,
Just stop and wave, they'll know you're near.

The Lure of Soft Sunshine

The sun peeks out with cheeky flair,
A golden wink, a loving stare.
It tickles blooms with rays so bright,
And makes them giggle in delight.

A bunny hops across the scene,
Chasing shadows, quick and keen.
It stops to sniff a daisy's head,
Then hops away, the flower's bred.

Oh, how the flowers bend and sway,
Like children at a game of play.
They shake their heads as if to say,
"Come join us in this bright ballet!"

The sun conspires with petals bold,
To weave a tale that's sweetly told.
Of laughter spun in warm embrace,
A sunny day, a playful space.

Hidden Reveries of the Earth

Beneath the soil, a party brews,
With roots and worms sporting bright hues.
The daisies gossip, quite absurd,
While crickets sing, not a word heard.

A tiny seed whispers, "I'm shy!"
"Just wait, my friend! You're meant to fly."
And off it goes, into the light,
To join the flowers, oh what a sight!

The earth can hold such wild dreams,
Of dancing petals and sunlit beams.
Where every bud has tales to share,
Of hidden joys beyond compare.

So if you listen, lean in near,
You'll catch a laugh or even cheer.
For down below, the earth underfoot,
Is filled with magic, oh so cute!

Blooming Beneath the Stars

At night, the garden takes a breath,
With twinkling lights like a ballet's death.
The flowers yawn and stretch out wide,
In moonlit robes, they take great pride.

A cricket band strikes up a tune,
While fireflies flash like little moons.
The flowers sway, they twist and spin,
Their petals shining—where to begin?

"Let's play hide and seek!" one daisy shouts,
And all agree, amid giggling bouts.
They hide behind the blades of grass,
A game of bloom, no need to pass.

So if you gaze at night's bright art,
And hear soft whispers in your heart,
Remember flowers dance and dream,
In secret worlds, with laughter's gleam.

Nature's Gentle Caress

In the garden, bugs dance a jig,
Making friends with a plump, pink pig.
Butterflies giggle as they fly near,
A squirrel snickers, clutching a beer.

Daisies sway to the tune of the wind,
While grasshoppers chirp, feeling quite pinned.
The daisies complain of a stubborn bee,
Whose buzzing is loud as a rap on TV.

While sunlight tickles the dew on the ground,
The flowers all laugh without making a sound.
The sun just grins, with rays so bright,
Chasing away shadows, causing a fright.

Oh, nature's a show, full of laughter and glee,
Even the trees twist their branches in spree.
So every petal, every leaf, every funny,
Whispers secrets of life, sweet and sunny.

Threads of Light in the Garden

A spider spun webs with elegant flair,
Caught a fly, but said, "Not a care!"
As bees in tuxedos buzz through the day,
The roses just roll as the daisies sway.

Sunshine pours in, a bright golden flood,
While worms groove wildly beneath the mud.
They wiggle and giggle, a wormy parade,
While the tulips all watch, but not dismayed.

In the distance, a gopher makes a scene,
Wearing his hat, looking quite mean.
Chasing shadows, he trips on a root,
And all the pansies stare in pursuit.

Threads of light weave tales in the air,
Nature's own comedy, if you dare.
Between rays and roots, laughter takes flight,
Dancing through petals, a whimsical sight.

A Heartfelt Bloom

A daffodil blushes, feeling so shy,
While a peony twirls, saying, "Oh my!"
A tulip sings loudly, out of tune,
As lilacs roll eyes, avoiding the moon.

Mice hold a concert under the stars,
Playing tiny violins, oh so bizarre!
The roses throw petals like confetti bright,
Laughing at critters who dance through the night.

A bumblebee jokes, "I'm late for my date!"
As the daisies respond, "Oh, isn't that great?"
Everyone chuckles, a riotous crew,
In this garden where giggles bloom new.

Under the moon, shady whispers are shared,
With secrets and laughter, no heart feels scared.
So each little flower, with humor's sweet plume,
Grins wide in the garden, a heartfelt bloom.

Secrets Linger Between the Leaves

The ferns whisper gossip without any fuss,
While violets giggle, "Did you catch that bus?"
A hedgehog rolls by in a fluffy grey coat,
As the pansies snicker and plot a new vote.

Beneath the oak, squirrels exchange winks,
As dandelions ponder on life's quirky links.
The grass blades chuckle at a bumble's blunder,
While the moon plays peek-a-boo, rolling with wonder.

Oh, hidden friendships, like treasures unseen,
In a wild game of tag where all can convene.
Each leaf holds a secret, delightful and sly,
Nature's own comics painted in the sky.

So roam through the garden, let laughter be found,
Where whimsy and nature create magic unbound.
A chorus of colors with mischief in sprees,
As secrets linger between each playful breeze.

Embracing the Shadowed Corners

In the corners where shadows creep,
Dust bunnies dance while we all sleep.
Who knew corners could be so bold?
They whisper secrets, stories untold.

A kitty pounces, feeling spry,
Chasing dust motes that drift by.
Laughter echoes as they collide,
In the shadows, where giggles abide.

Corners hold pots of gold,
Or at least stories that never get old.
Through the curtains they tease and peep,
In the shadows, we find joy so deep.

The Promise of New Life

From cracked pots come sprouts of green,
With a wink and nudge, they convene.
Little shoots stretch out and yawn,
Poking through fences, all at dawn.

What's this? A flower in a shoe?
Is it nature or a prankster's cue?
With blooms and laughter, life's a show,
They giggle as they learn and grow.

Each sprout a promise — silly and bold,
Sprouting tales that never grow old.
Nature chuckles as seeds take flight,
In the garden, everything feels just right.

Mornings Wrapped in Color

Sunrise paints the world so bright,
With splashes of orange, pink, and light.
Birds are chirping, joining the spree,
Coffee's brewing — the day's jubilee!

A dog in pajamas runs round the yard,
Accidentally tripping, it's not so hard.
Neighbors peep from behind their drapes,
As morning unfolds in all its shapes.

With each sip, smiles grow wide,
In this colorful chaos, we all confide.
Mornings wrapped in hues so bright,
Hold laughter and missteps in pure delight.

Secrets Held in Petal's Fold

Petals whisper tales so sweet,
In their folds, secrets meet.
A butterfly pauses, curious and sly,
Listening close as dreams float by.

What happens in gardens stays quite hush,
Gossiping blooms hide in the brush.
With whispers of love and laughter too,
They hold onto joy like morning dew.

In the fold of each petal's grace,
Lies a giggle, a wink, a twinkling face.
Nature's own comedy, secrets sown,
In petals' embrace, we're never alone.

Cradled by Nature's Touch

Among flowers dancing, bees wear a grin,
Tickled by breezes, let the laughter begin.
Silly sunflowers, heads held up high,
Whispering secrets as butterflies fly.

Birds serenade with a comical tweet,
While squirrels debate their acorn retreat.
In the garden of giggles, life writes a plot,
Nature's own humor, piping warm and hot.

Rabbits in bowties, a curious sight,
Napping on daisies, still in delight.
Petunia's perfume wafts through the air,
Each whiff a chuckle, inviting a stare.

So here's to the joy that blooms all around,
Where laughter and nature are easily found.
Join in the frolic, let worries float,
On this merry journey, we'll happily gloat.

The Dance of Soft Light

When twilight giggles and paints the sky,
Fireflies pop up with a zesty hi!
Crickets compose tunes that tickle your ears,
While stars do the cha-cha, silencing fears.

In the glow of the moon, shadows prance and play,
Mice in their overcoats, mucking about in ballet.
As sparkling dust swirls, the night feels alive,
With a dance of soft light, we all start to thrive.

Laughter echoes through the serene night air,
While giggling leaves sway without a care.
Each glow seems to giggle, casting a spell,
In this wacky waltz where all creatures dwell.

So when daylight wanes and the fun begins,
Join the whimsical dance, let the night's joy win.
Under the starry blanket, let your spirit take flight,
In the dance of soft light, everything feels right.

A Symphony of Colors

In a garden explosion, colors collide,
Where oranges and purples seem to take pride.
Tickling the noses of passerby folks,
Each petal a giggle, each stem a good joke.

Amidst the green, a dandelion yodels,
While pansies wear spectacles, laughing like models.
A rainbow of chuckles, bright as can be,
Nature's own buffet of joyful decree.

Hummingbirds hover, playing tag with the sun,
While blooms toss confetti, 'Oh, what fun!'
A splash here, a dash there, chaos, but grand,
In this vibrant embrace, everything's planned.

So let's paint our hearts with this symphony bright,
Where colors giggle, and days feel just right.
Join in the riddle, where nature unfolds,
A masterpiece of humor, in vibrant golds.

Breathing Life into Dreams

In a meadow of winks, the breeze does insist,
Air filled with tickles, you can't help but twist.
Clouds play peek-a-boo with the curious trees,
While daisies chime softly, 'Come dance with ease.'

Rainbow-fish frolic in whispers of streams,
While frogs croak their wishes, turning dreams into beams.
With a wink and a nudge, the daisies all cheer,
'Life's silly and sweet, so why scowl in fear?'

Glimmers of laughter weave through the night,
As shadows play tag with the soft morning light.
Each petal unwinds, a comic relief,
Breathing dreams anew, with heartbeats of belief.

So let's spin our tales, oh, turn up the glee,
In this bright open world, there's joy guaranteed.
With dreams that are giggling and hearts fluttering free,
We breathe in life's magic, just you wait and see!

Enchanted by Soft Hues

In a garden full of cheer,
Colors dance, oh so near.
Little blooms in every corner,
Whisper secrets, a delight for the mourner.

Bumblebees with tiny hats,
Buzz around like chatty spats.
Daisies giggle, tulips tease,
Petals flutter in the breeze.

Sunlight sprinkles, oh so bright,
Flowers open with pure delight.
Even weeds in festive dress,
Come together in gentle mess.

Amidst the fun, a squirrel prances,
Thinking it's winning flower glances.
A bouquet of laughs in vibrant hues,
Tickling noses, and silly shoes.

Sunlit Hopes

Under the sun's warm embrace,
Frolics spring, a merry chase.
Silken petals do a jig,
In this world where joy's not big.

The daisies play hopscotch tight,
While the roses twirl, what a sight!
Napping bees dream of sweet cake,
In a garden, where fun's no mistake.

A sunflower winks at the bowers,
Laughing at clouds with sticky showers.
Dandelion wishes float so free,
Giggles echo, come join me!

Butterflies in crazy trails,
Chase the wind, set their sails.
Nature teases in vibrant schemes,
Whispers of joy dance in dreams.

Beneath a Gentle Sky

Beneath the azure canopy,
Nature's gags, pure comedy.
A frog croaks, trying to croon,
Join the beat, sing a tune!

Forget-me-not in sassy pairs,
Make it clear, they're not for shares.
Petal fights and pollen spat,
It's a circus, imagine that!

Dancing shadows play peek-a-boo,
With daisies in a raucous queue.
Clouds giggle as they drift on by,
Like fluffy children, no reason why.

Dancing grass, following the beat,
Brush against shoes as springtime greets.
Laughter hidden in leafy nooks,
More fun than thrilling books.

The Language of Blooming

In every bloom, a joke is spun,
Nature's laughter, never done.
Pansies wear their silly frowns,
Blossoms toss out giggly crowns.

A rose rolls eyes at the grass,
"Why do you always let weeds pass?"
Snapdragons chat with cheeky flair,
Turning heads everywhere.

With each sunrise, hilarity grows,
Buds opening in funny clothes.
Fluffy seeds in frolics scatter,
Making sure, nothing's the matter.

In this riot of vibrant chuckles,
Life blooms with mischievous snuggles.
Whispers of joy among the vines,
In a land where laughter shines.

Awakening the Spirit of Nature

In the garden, bugs all prance,
Mice dance wildly, take a chance.
Squirrels chatter, trees will sway,
Nature's party, come and play!

With a giggle, raindrops fall,
Bouncing off the leaves so tall.
Frogs are croaking their delight,
Celebrating day to night!

Sunbeams tickle every flower,
Making friends with bees each hour.
As daisies wear their sunny hats,
Nature's knocking - where are the cats?

So let's join this wild parade,
Find a spot and laugh, cascade!
In the joyful, sunny clime,
Nature's antics, oh so prime!

The Light in a Flower's Heart

Inside a bloom, there's quite a show,
Bees wear costumes, putting on a glow.
Petals twirl like tiny skirts,
Nature's dance – no room for blurts!

Ladybugs in tuxedos bright,
Waltzing under the soft moonlight.
A rogue snail crashes the big ball,
And trips just as he makes his call!

The lilies giggle, the roses tease,
While daisies play a game of freeze.
"Who's the best dancer?" they all shout,
In nature's cabaret, there's no doubt!

So stop and watch this lively spree,
Flowers laugh with such pure glee.
Join the fun, don't be shy,
Come on out, give it a try!

When Colors Blossom

When colors bloom, the world takes flight,
Crayons spill, what a sight!
Pinks and yellows start to blend,
Nature's palette has no end!

Fluffy clouds with cotton candy flair,
Butterflies are everywhere.
Flowers giggle in full bloom,
It's a carnival, make some room!

Chasing rainbows through the day,
Every hue has come to play.
Even grass gets a little wild,
Celebrating like a care-free child!

So come and twirl in this riot of hue,
Dance with the flowers, just me and you.
In a world full of giggles and glee,
Where colors blossom, wild and free!

Dreams of a Starry Evening

Under stars, the crickets sing,
What a strange, delightful thing.
Moonbeams twinkle, sprightly play,
Nighttime mischief on display!

Fireflies wear their tiny hats,
Generating giggles from the bats.
A hedgehog whispers tales of woe,
Until a curious owl says, "No!"

Wishing stars play peek-a-boo,
While shadows dance, the breeze is new.
Twirling leaves, a midnight chase,
Nature's giggles all in place!

So dream beneath this starry dome,
With the critters, make a home.
In the laughter of the night,
Find the joy, let spirits light!

The Gentle Touch of Time

Time tickles us with its charms,
Like squirrels stealing unguarded farms.
It dances lightly, never late,
Making plans with fate.

With every laugh, it slips away,
A naughty game we love to play.
We chase shadows, oh what fun,
While time just winks and runs.

It draws us in with a sly grin,
Leaving tales of where we've been.
In cozy corners, it takes a seat,
Playing tricks, oh what a feat!

So let us giggle at its tricks,
As moments pass like magic flicks.
For in this dance, both sweet and sly,
We'll share our laughs before goodbye.

A Whisper Carried by the Wind

The wind whispers secrets, oh so sweet,
It tickles your nose, then retreats.
It lifts your hat, gives a cheeky shout,
While leaves go swirling about.

Dandelions laugh as they take flight,
Floating around, a whimsical sight.
Each gentle puff carries a glee,
As the wind plays hide and seek with me.

A banter of breezes, silly and bold,
Sharing tales of springtime gold.
With every gust, a giggle's spun,
In the dance of joy under the sun.

So let the whispers fill the air,
With laughter and jests to share.
For in this game, so light and free,
The wind's our friend, just wait and see.

The Fabric of Spring

In springtime fabrics, colors collide,
A patchwork quilt where smiles reside.
With blossoms stitched in cheerful tones,
And laughter woven into our bones.

Grass tickles toes in a playful spree,
While squirrels debate on what's next for tea.
A tapestry spun with warmth and cheer,
As nature dons its favorite gear.

Sunshine agreements with clouds that giggle,
Creating rainbows that twist and wiggle.
A humorous dance of weather's whim,
With nature's laughter spilling from the brim.

So come join in this merry thread,
Where whimsy and wonder widely spread.
In each stitch, a promise rings,
In the fabric of spring, life happily sings.

Unfurling Dreams in the Quiet

In the quiet moments, dreams take flight,
Like sleepy kittens in the night.
They stretch and yawn, ready to play,
As they chase the shadows away.

With each soft whisper, hopes awake,
A secret dance that clouds often shake.
Silently giggling, they find their place,
In the hidden corners of time and space.

A flutter here, a twirl there,
Dreams giggle softly, filling the air.
In the stillness, they spread their wings,
Creating laughter from simple things.

So let us listen to the hush,
Where dreams unfold in playful rush.
For in that quiet, we all share,
The joy of dreaming, light as air.

The Dancer's Footprint in the Garden

In the garden where laughter grows,
A dancer twirls with silly toes.
Each stamp leaves blooms, a vibrant show,
Even daisies giggle in their rows.

She leaps and hops, so full of glee,
Not a care for the buzzing bee.
While worms are rolling, trying to flee,
A comedy act for all to see!

Her clumsy shuffle shakes the ground,
Stepping on the petals, round and round.
The tulips cheer, the roses abound,
As the breeze plays merry tunes, profound.

But when she stumbles, oh, what a sight!
The clouds turn purple, the sun takes flight.
Together they giggle till night,
In this wacky, whimsical delight.

Sentiments of a Gentle Breeze

A breeze swirls through the laughing trees,
Brushing past in playful tease.
It tickles leaves and rolls in ease,
Whispers secrets, fluffing bees.

In its wake, the petals swirl,
Flower hats spun with a twirl.
The garden sings, a merry pearl,
As the wind gives nature a twirl.

The breeze chuckles, no time to stall,
Pushing daisies, one and all.
It lifts a squirrel, oh what a sprawl,
Even the pines seem to enthrall!

Gliding onward, it winks and bows,
Causing laughter under boughs.
Leaves rustle, as if to vow,
Endless giggles in the now.

New Beginnings at Twilight

The sun sets low, shadows prance,
In twilight's glow, the flowers dance.
Buds pop open with a glance,
Whispering secrets of romance.

At twilight's peak, the crickets sing,
Making plans for a night of fling.
Fireflies glow, a dazzling bling,
While moonbeams chuckle, warm and spring.

A flower yawns, its petals fold,
Inviting stars, bright and bold.
Underneath, the stories told,
Of nightly dreams and joy untold.

And as the night takes center stage,
Each leaf turns—an eager page.
In this dance, no hint of rage,
Just giggles grow, at every age.

Secrets of the Soil

Down below where the critters play,
The soil chuckles, come what may.
With worms and roots, they form a sway,
Telling tales in their earthy play.

"Oh, what secrets do we hold?"
Says the compost, wise and old.
With each laugh, a story told,
Of adventures far and bold.

The beetles march in clever lines,
Stomping rhythms, as if in signs.
A concert grand among the vines,
While hidden treasures shyly shine.

Underneath, the fun won't cease,
Nature's party, a jaunty feast.
Beneath our feet, such joy released,
In every root, a giggle teased.

The Dance of Sunlit Flora

In the garden, petals twirl,
With bees who dance and swirl.
They sip the nectar sweet,
Doing their little beet retreat.

A ladybug in polka dots,
Sipping tea with friendly thoughts.
They gossip 'neath the sunny blaze,
In this floral cabaret maze.

The daisies poke their heads up high,
Winking at the clouds up in the sky.
The daisies, they can't seem to tell,
Who's funnier? The flowers or the shell?

As petals fall, the laughter swells,
With every giggle, charm compels.
For every bloom has got a joke,
In this riot of flowers, laughter broke.

Threads of Grace in Soft Earth

In the earth where secrets hide,
Worms and roots enjoy the ride.
They twine and twist, a silly sight,
Dancing quietly into the night.

The daisies in their finest dress,
Tease the grass, Oh what a mess!
With ribbons made of verdant lace,
They race around, it's quite the chase.

The tulips boast their velvet hues,
While snails debate the best of views.
In earthy tones and playful cheer,
They laugh at flowers soaring near.

Each bloom's a thread, a lively song,
Weaving tales where roots belong.
In this garden, the giggles spread,
Chasing worries, leaving dread.

A Garden of Unspoken Oaths

In this patch of wild delight,
Every flower has a secret bite.
The violets whisper, full of glee,
A jest shared quietly 'neath the tree.

With rain on leaves, a ticklish sound,
While petunias spread their smiles around.
Sunflowers stand tall, making faces,
While ants march on in silly paces.

Busy bees in their buzzing chat,
Plotting mischief, imagine that!
With every bloom a hidden jest,
In a garden where we all feel blessed.

Lilies keep a diary of fun,
With each new tale, they feel undone.
For in this sacred, cactus-studded dream,
Laughter echoes, or so it seems!

The Quiet Bloom of Affection

Amidst the greens where silence stirs,
A bloom unfurls with gentle purrs.
Petals as soft as childhood lore,
Whisper sweet secrets, wanting more.

A stubborn bud gives a cheeky wink,
As earthworms plot their next little chink.
In this patch, all worries cease,
As blossoms gather, finding peace.

The roses chase the laughter and smiles,
While thorns enjoy the long, silly trials.
With cheeky blooms and a teasing breeze,
This garden's a stage that aims to please.

Where each bloom tells a tale unique,
Of love, of laughter, and playful mystique.
In the quiet blooms of affection's light,
Every petal giggles, shining bright.

Starlit Soliloquies in the Meadow

Under the moon, the critters dance,
A rabbit hops, caught in a trance.
Fireflies flicker with cheeky glee,
Whispering secrets to the tall grass and me.

The owl hoots jokes, like a stand-up pro,
While crickets click their heels, putting on a show.
In this whimsy, laughter fills the air,
Nature's comedy, beyond compare.

The daisies gossip about a sly beetle,
Who thinks he's the king, but lacks a single medal.
With petals a-twitter and leaves a-chatter,
It's a raucous league of jovial matter.

So sit back and giggle, let worries decay,
In the starlit meadow, come join the play.
For the night is young, and laughter's a must,
Under twinkling stars, in nature we trust.

Heartbeats of Petals in the Breezes

The flowers sway with a hip-hop beat,
As breezes bring gossip, oh so sweet.
Petal hearts flutter, can you believe?
They're whispering stories of tricks up their sleeve.

Dandelions puff with a proud little grin,
Claiming their crowns, it's a scandalous win.
While tulips twirl in their frilly array,
Chasing the wind, come out to play!

The bees bumble loudly, their dance full of flair,
Acting like royalty, without a care.
In this floral fiesta, silly laughs bloom,
Every corner presents a new fragrant room.

So skip through the petals, let your heart race,
Each breeze brings a smile, a delightful embrace.
With joy all around, and laughter anew,
Petals will bounce, creating a funny view.

Beneath the Blossoms of Tomorrow

Under the blossoms, oh what a sight!
A squirrel slips, taking a wild flight.
The flowers giggle, they can't help themselves,
As leaves recount tales from the highest shelves.

The sun's warm rays play hide and seek,
While a worm sings songs, oh so oblique.
Beneath the buds where mischief is bred,
Laughter erupts, where no worries are fed.

Chirping birds offer their humorous news,
While daisies wear their bright Sunday shoes.
Every bloom's a jester, in this vibrant spree,
Tickling the skies with laughter and glee!

So gather your giggles, let's swing by the trees,
In the shade of laughter, with a ticklish breeze.
For tomorrow's bright blooms will dance in delight,
Creating a symphony from the day till the night.

In the Shade of Whispering Leaves

In the leafy lounge, the breezes sway,
Where leafy whispers have something to say.
The trees tell tales in their rustling voice,
Inviting all critters to come and rejoice.

A snail slips by with a glimmering grin,
While a beetle brags, saying, 'I can spin!'
Laughter erupts from the boughs overhead,
As a squirrel somersaults, bold as he's bred.

The rhubarb chuckles, it can't keep a secret,
Offering up jokes, as wit takes a leap.
While the daisies chuckle, in slow-motion grace,
They giggle and twist in a floral embrace.

So nestle beneath and let chuckles unfold,
In the shade of laughter, where stories are told.
With each playful breeze and each tickling tease,
We dance with the leaves amid joyful decrees.

Twilight's Gentle Bloom

In the twilight where flowers grin,
Bees in a dance, let the fun begin.
A squirrel in a top hat, oh what a sight,
Swings from the branches, taking flight.

Petals that tickle, what a great tease,
Laughter among daisies sways in the breeze.
A robin's joke makes the sunbeam sing,
While shadows play hide and seek in spring.

Traces of Joy in the Garden

Among the blooms, a giggle might sprout,
Where veggies wear coats, oh what's that about?
Tomatoes in shades of rosy delight,
Holding a tea party under moonlight.

Carrots with capes, they run with such grace,
While the lettuce blinks in a game of chase.
A cucumber slips, oh the ruckus begins,
Who knew the garden had such silly spins?

Soft Hues of a New Dawn

Morning breaks with a giggle and yawn,
Sunflowers stretch, their faces now drawn.
While marigolds whisper, secrets to share,
   A butterfly wiggles, floats in midair.

With dew on their petals, they shimmer and shine,
   As ladybugs waltz in a fancy line.
Chasing the clouds, they dance 'round the sun,
   A lively garden, where folly is fun.

Beneath the Canopy of Kinship

Under the trees where the giggles collide,
Families of blooms share joy with pride.
Pansies poke fun, teasing the leaves,
As dandelions blow, making wishes with ease.

In corners they chuckle, bright petals aglow,
A family of flora, all putting on a show.
With vines intertwining, they whisper and plot,
Creating a circus from what they've got.

Echoed Laughter in the Fields

In fields where daisies dream and nod,
A goat with style took off his clod.
He pranced and danced, without a care,
While chickens laughed, with feathers in their hair.

The sun played tricks, peeked through the trees,
As bees tried to hum their B-flat with ease.
A rabbit popped up, doing a jig,
Challenging the world to join the big gig.

With each loud giggle, clouds rolled away,
As frogs in tuxedos croaked their ballet.
The laughter spread far on the warm, soft breeze,
Every bloom joined in, had their own tease.

So if you wander where the chuckles grow,
Watch for the fun, the silly show.
For in this land of laughter and glee,
Even the flowers dance full of spree.

A Melody in the Meadow

In a meadow bright, where the sunbeams flirt,
A squirrel donned gloves, wore a tiny shirt.
He waltzed with the daisies, twirled with delight,
Singing off-key 'til it fell into night.

The bumblebees buzzed, holding a tune,
While frogs in a chorus croaked to the moon.
With wiggles and giggles, they joined in a throng,
Creating a symphony, silly and strong.

But just as the show reached a peak of its cheer,
A wind gusted wildly, making them fear.
Their notes scattered wildly, high up in the sky,
Like popcorn bursting, oh my, oh my!

Yet laughter returned as they danced on the ground,
With hiccups and snickers, no frowns to be found.
So heed this tune, let your joy be set free,
Life's melody blooms in the heart of the spree.

The Soft Breath of Spring

Spring whispered sweetly, with a giggle and glide,
As flowers awoke, each one blushing with pride.
A tulip declared it was time to break free,
While daffodils chuckled in glee by the sea.

A butterfly stammered, 'Is this all a dream?'
As snails rolled in laughter, they formed quite a team.
With socks on their shells, they slid down the lane,
Turning puddles to joy, oh what a gain!

The sun poured its warmth, like lemonade bright,
Bringing giggles and smiles, pure joy in the light.
An ant donned a hat, declaring a fair,
Inviting all critters, they danced everywhere.

As laughter exploded, the flowers stood tall,
Competing for jokes to enchant one and all.
So take a deep breath, feel the soft springtime zing,
And listen for laughter; it's the best kind of thing.

Reflections in a Dewdrop

In a dewdrop's shimmer, a world spun anew,
Frogs held a council, all dressed in their blue.
They pondered the weather, who'd jump first, they dreamed,
As laughter erupted, bursting at the seams.

An owl wearing glasses proclaimed, 'It's my turn!'
As bugs roared with laughter, in excitement they churned.

Each drop held a vision, of whimsy and fun,
Their giggle was brighter than the morning sun.

A snail told a tale of a race he once lost,
The rabbits just howled, 'Hey, was it worth the cost?'
With a splash of delight, a squirrel chased his hat,
Creating a whirl, oh what a spiffy spat!

So gaze in the drop, see the joy that it shows,
For laughter is boundless, like weeds, it just grows.
In tiny reflections, life dances along,
With humor as sweet as an old, funny song.

Whispers of Spring's Awakening

The flowers giggle under the sun,
They whisper secrets, oh what fun!
Bees start buzzing, taking a dive,
Nature's party, let's come alive!

Chirping birds draw a funny tune,
Dancing shadows beneath the moon.
Silly squirrels in a fancy race,
Chasing tails, oh, what a chase!

With every bloom, a jest unfolds,
Petal-friends sharing jokes untold.
Buds are blushing, bright and spry,
Winking at passers, oh my, oh my!

In the garden, mischief's afoot,
Twirling leaves in their playful route.
Spring laughs loudly, not hiding its zest,
Nature's laughter is simply the best!

Blooming Beneath the Frost

Amidst the ice, a flower's grin,
A stubborn bloom, let the fun begin!
With petals bright, in winter's frock,
It pokes fun at the chilly clock.

Snowflakes tickle, like little friends,
As winter grumbles, spring just bends.
With cozy coats, they giggle tight,
Frosty jokes make the cold feel right.

Daffodils chuckle, sipping hot tea,
Dressed in white, oh so comically!
They snicker softly, sharing the wild,
At winter's joke, they're nature's child.

Through frosted nights, humor's the star,
Blooming bravely, like a quirk from afar.
In this chilly land, laughter prevails,
Frosty tales hold the warmth in trails!

Vows of the Golden Petals

Golden petals, a vow we make,
To dance in sunlight, for laughter's sake.
With every swish, they speak a word,
Promises of joy, that's how they're stirred.

In the meadow, a buzzing crowd,
Flowers form oaths, funny and loud.
Tickling each other with lavender's tease,
Whispers of humor carried by the breeze.

Bees hold meetings, in petals grand,
Discussing plans, all perfectly planned.
With pollen jokes, they buzz and sway,
These golden blooms keep dullness at bay.

When sunshine wakes and stretches wide,
Laughter spills forth, there's nothing to hide.
In the garden of giggles, a fun parade,
Golden petals dance, never afraid!

Secrets Carried by the Breeze

Whispers float on a playful breeze,
Tickling flowers, joking with ease.
Leaves giggle softly, their laughter tight,
Secrets of spring, they know what's right.

A dandelion tells a corny joke,
While nearby tulips giggle and poke.
Jokes about bees that can't quite fly,
Swirling in circles, oh my, oh my!

As butterflies flutter, they join the fun,
Spreading laughter 'til the day is done.
Each secret carried, a comical gift,
In nature's laughter, our spirits lift.

So next time you stroll through blooms and trees,
Listen closely to the whispered tease.
For every flower has laughter to share,
Secrets of joy float softly in the air!

Dreams Nestled in Blooming Valleys

In valleys where the daisies play,
Dreams are lost and found each day.
Bumblebees with dance so grand,
Making friends in sunbeam land.

A tulip tells a joke or two,
While lilies giggle, oh so blue.
Sunshine spills like lemonade,
As laughter echoes, unafraid.

Petals twirl in breezy fun,
Chasing shadows, everyone.
With roots that tickle, grass that sings,
In this garden, joy takes wings.

So let your dreams take flight today,
In blooming valleys, come what may.
For laughter sprouts where flowers grow,
In silly dances, love will show.

The Heart of a Flowering Wish

A daisied heart beats loud and clear,
With petals whispering, never fear.
Tulips gossip in the sun,
While pansies say, let's have some fun!

A dandelion chases the breeze,
Playing tag with bumblebees.
With every bloom, a wish takes flight,
In a garden filled with pure delight.

Roses wink in bright array,
Sharing secrets of the day.
Every bud has tales to tell,
In this floral wishing well.

So let your laughter grow and spread,
Among the blooms, where joy is bred.
The heart of wonder never fades,
In gardens where our fun cascades.

Whispers of the Dawn

As dawn breaks with a giggle and yawn,
Morning glories stretch, oh how they fawn.
With each stretch, the world awakes,
In fields where laughter softly quakes.

A rooster clucks a silly tune,
While butterflies dance 'neath the moon.
In the chorus of a new day's start,
The whispers of joy fill every heart.

Dew drops gleam like diamonds bright,
They splatter dreams in morning light.
Silly birds wear hats of grass,
As giggles float and moments pass.

Whispers flutter on the breeze,
Painting smiles on waking trees.
So join the fun as day unfolds,
In nature's arms, warmth it holds.

In the Garden of Dreams

In a garden where wild imaginations bloom,
Silly gnomes chase away the gloom.
With mushrooms that giggle and sway,
Every moment is a fun buffet!

Tulips prance in colors bright,
While daisies throw a joyful fight.
Laughter echoes and butterflies spin,
In the dance of joy, let's all join in!

Fairy tales blossom on every stem,
While hedgehogs play a hidden gem.
With flowers telling jokes galore,
No dull moment in this folklore!

Join the fun, let worry cease,
In a garden that breathes pure peace.
With every petal, let's explore,
In the garden of dreams, forevermore.

www.ingramcontent.com/pod-product-compliance
Lightning Source LLC
Chambersburg PA
CBHW051644160426
43209CB00004B/790